Pink Crosses

Roy Mitchell

Copyright © 2013 Roy Mitchell

All rights reserved.

ISBN-13: 978-1493716470
ISBN-10: 1493716476

For Suzette

Chapter 1

"Oh, God!" Suzette exclaimed into her cell phone.

I knew as soon as the words left her mouth. The call brought bad news, really bad news.

Easing off the pedal, I coasted into a parking lot. The biopsy results were in. We'd been expecting them. Suzette's pencil and a piece of paper already sat on the console between the seats. She grabbed them, writing quickly. In the middle of the page, my wife of nineteen years scribbled, "breast cancer."

Neither word was capitalized. There wasn't even an exclamation point or an underline. They were just there, like any other two words you could scribble on a page – two six-letter words that would change our lives.

I admired Suzette's reaction. It was like she skipped over the stage of immediate weeping. In an instant, my wife was perfectly composed. In the seat next to her, I had just started falling apart.

Our minivan straddled two or three empty parking spaces next to Coosa High School. The school still teemed with students - the band, the football team, cheerleaders. All those plus a couple of other groups peppered the other side of campus. Underneath a row of trees, this parking lot was practically abandoned by 4:00 every day. If I hadn't been in tears, I would have thought the surroundings quite peaceful. I wiped my face.

After writing the words, "breast cancer," Suzette asked the nurse as calmly and as clearly as if she'd been asking directions at a street corner, "What do we do now?" The nurse had no way of fully answering such a question. It's not her fault. She could schedule appointments, interpret test results, and counsel Suzette. The nurse couldn't tell us answers we really wanted to know. Does this mean chemotherapy? What about radiation? Will her hair fall out? How sick will she become? For me all questions revolved around a single thought – what are Suzette's chances of survival?

The conversation took about fifteen minutes. As clear-headed as a glass mannequin, Suzette took notes. She would likely need surgery. Before then, a myriad of appointments, tests, and counseling awaited. Jotted scribbles invaded the paper like kudzu on a hillside. Notes of possible treatments, diet suggestions, and appointment times completely engulfed the centered words, "breast cancer." If only the disease could be surrounded and consumed so easily.

Then I saw the note page from a different perspective. The words "breast cancer" suddenly became sympathetic. Instead of being lonely in the center of the page, all Suzette's notes surrounded them and kept them company. It's funny how the brain works. Maybe my mind was preparing itself for a journey of both fighting and feeling.

I can't count the number of times I cried the rest of the phone call. I fought tears the entire time and then some. Through the distortion of my wet eye cavities, I spied most every note and eavesdropped what I could. Tears sometimes left their sockets and streamed downward. Other times they retreated, only to return to their launching points in the corners and along the bottom rims of my eyelids.

The ultrasound revealed four cancerous masses in Suzette's right breast. Three of them appeared close together and were considered one "lump." It stretched over five centimeters in length. The fourth was alone – in the same breast, but not near the other cancerous mass. Her doctor would be back in town in three weeks. That's when surgery would likely take place.

Suzette eventually ran out of questions. The nurse wished my wife good luck. Suzette closed her cell phone. Thus began what I knew might be the longest three weeks of our lives.

Suzette and I have two children. Alex is a sixteen, and Zac is twelve. Zac heard the news as I heard the news. He was sitting in the back seat during the conversation. During the call I remembered having checked on Zac through my rear view mirror. The gravity of the conversation was on his face. He wasn't crying, but he was deeply concerned. To keep my own composure I had turned my eyes away.

Within moments of hanging up, Suzette's maternal instincts kicked in. She immediately thought to reassure Zac.

Suzette opened the van door and stepped out. She pulled the side-door lever. It opened. Zac was there. My wife instantly took his hands, confronting his fears. She said,

"Zac, this doesn't mean that I'm going to die. Lots and lots of people survive breast cancer."

I ineffectively tried to contribute, mustering the words, "Lots and lots. There are lots of people, Zac." My face began to tighten as tears succumbed to gravity. I let Suzette do the rest of the talking.

My son returned her stare with a petrified look. He was still too scared to respond. Suzette filled in the void quickly, saying, "I have waited all my life to raise you boys." Her voice began to crack. She pulled it together, continuing, "We're going to fight this, and we're going to win."

Her resolve as well as her words won Zac over. They hugged in a long embrace. Zac said a heartfelt, "I love you, Mom."

A few moments later I put the van in drive. We eased out of the parking lot toward the rest of our lives, not sure exactly where the road would take us.

I'll never forget the heart-wrenching quarter of an hour from 4:00 to 4:15 pm September 20, 2013. Ironically, I may never remember what happened from 4:15-5:00 that Friday. We probably turned left out of the parking lot and rode toward town. We may have even gone to a store. Perhaps we just drove around. I don't recall. Some time before our oldest son got out of band practice, I phoned and told my mother the news. Wherever we went and whatever else happened, we ended up back at Coosa High School just after 5:00.

At age 45 I'm getting older, but my memory's not normally that bad. The incident kind of reminds me of a Sequoia tree. You know, they're those super-sized trees you sometimes find out California. I've never been there, but when I was a kid, I saw a photograph of one of them. The picture had this gigantic Sequoia tree. From its base emerged a road – yes, a road. The tree was so big that a hole had been cut out of its base. A road led up to it from either side. It was an eye-catching photo.

The focus of the photo is squarely on the gargantuan tree and the unexpected path belched from it. I'm surprised I remember the picture at all. What I don't recall, however, is any other details besides the tree and road. Were there any little bushes around the tree or fallen leaves, maybe? Perhaps a squirrel peeked sheepishly around the massive trunk then. I don't know. Other details of the picture faded into the lost recesses of my mind decades ago. Like the picture, fringe events of that hour after the phone call simply faded away, never to be remembered again.

Five-thirty came and went. A few minutes later, Alex and his tuba case appeared in the doorway of the band room. Our oldest son stands 6 feet 5 inches tall. He's fiercely proud of his stature. That and the fact that he can sport a healthy forest of chin hair leaves him feeling like the Big Man on Campus. Everyday reactions reveal a growing independence. More now than ever, he hides his emotions. It's that "I can deal with it myself," attitude for which teenagers are known. How would he react when we told him the news?

His tuba in tow, our eldest approached the van. We both met him at the trunk. I lifted the hatch for Alex's instrument. Suzette cleared out a space. Alex approached. She didn't mince words. Suzette looked up at him and said, "It's cancer." She nodded her head up and down, completing the thought, "I have breast cancer." I could feel the tears coming in my own eyes again. Batting them and turning my head away, I didn't see all the exchange. When I turned around, our eldest son's arms had already extended out.

This was the busy side of the school. Cars whisked past them, and dozens of people, maybe close to a hundred, were in sight, going about their daily teenage lives. For us, time stood still as mother and son embraced.

We shouldn't have eaten out that day. As Dave Ramsey would say, "There was too much month for the money."

Once we got in the van, Suzette spoke to her three sullen men, "Let's eat out!" In an unexpectedly cheerful tone, she exclaimed, "Let's celebrate that my cancer was caught early!" The boys nodded their approval.

Cancer was all I thought about on the ride there. I broke my diet for a pork burrito with cheese. It gave me indigestion.

Most weekends are the same. Suzette and I are teachers. I had schoolwork to do. She had schoolwork to do. Both boys had homework for the weekend. None of us even touched it that night.

We spent much of the time in the living room. Before long, boys opened their instrument cases and let the notes fly. The bleating bass of Alex's tuba and the shrill interjection of Zac's trumpet echoed through our house and probably well into the yard. Normally, Suzette and I shy away from the boys while they practice. Even one of them tooting their horn is almost too loud for one to bear. That night they played their horns together. It was loud and startling, carrying as much disharmony as one could imagine. We listened…and smiled…and pushed cancer to the back of our minds for a while.

Later on, Suzette meandered into our bed. I followed, leaving the boys to their musical merriment. We spoke a few words, and I left to retrieve my laptop. By the time I returned, the boys had abandoned their instruments, scurried into the bedroom, and had taken my place. Alex hopped on the bed first. Zac scurried in right after, leaping in between them. The waterbed rolled both Suzette and Alex away from the center and almost off the bed. Everyone all laughed. I sat down and watched the entire thing. After many more smiles and a few hugs, they finally dragged their tired bodies to bed.

When the boys left, we kept lights on. Both of us read in our Bibles before sleep conquered our consciousness.

I don't recall exactly what time I dozed. When a hand shook my shoulder, that time I remember. It was 12:09 am. For the first time Suzette felt fear. Her voice cracked. She had been crying. Through the emotion she said, "I'm scared."

I rolled over, holding her tight in the dark.

The next day was a Saturday. We slept late. It was raining. I had every reason to believe that the next three weeks would be as dreary and sullen as the weather outside. I knew I shouldn't feel that burdened. A mammogram just six months earlier had been deemed clear. Surely any cancerous cells couldn't have spread too far. There was great hope, even in the face of a cancer diagnosis. There was also room for fear. Cancer seemed like handling poisonous snakes. Even with great precautions, a snake still might kill you.

This cancer could be easily controlled, maybe even completely eliminated by surgery or radiation. On the other hand, the disease could leave our children without a mother. Fear breeds in an incomplete prognosis, and it creates an irony. Suzette's on most every prayer chain in two counties. To her students, she is the face of breast cancer. Even with such attention, there may be a better chance of Suzette dying of e-coli poisoning from roadrunner poop than from cancer.

In one of my science classes we recently covered the difference between kinetic energy and potential energy. I used the following example to explain the difference between the two.

A ball sitting at the top of a hill may not be moving. It's still considered to have a kind of energy - potential energy. The textbook calls it the energy of position. That ball sitting on top of a hill has a higher likelihood of moving than a ball sitting on flat land. It's only when the ball rolls downward that the potential energy is replaced with kinetic energy (energy of movement).

A person diagnosed with cancer is like the ball on top of the hill. Being close to a hill doesn't guarantee the ball from ever rolling down it. A person with cancer may live a very long life, not ever succumbing to the disease. Then again, the ball may drop quickly. In waiting those three weeks, we can't help but look down the hill. We see the valley of the shadow of death, hoping Suzette's health doesn't start rolling toward it.

Thinking about it too much tends to make you panic. A similar panic during that time reminded me of that.

One Saturday during those three weeks I took Zac to all-state chorus try-outs at a nearby high school. I should've known when I pulled into the parking lot. It was dripping with cars like a sponge full of water. We finally parked in a space about a quarter of a mile away.

My boy was supposed to perform in front of the judges at 11:39. The directors recommended we arrive thirty minutes early. We were forty minutes early, even with the long walk from a distant parking lot. The precise time and our promptness encouraged me that we would be in and out in short order. I couldn't have been more wrong.

Three hours later, Zac still wasn't finished. I was fine until I wandered back into the building. That's when I encountered a fidgety dad. He had approached a worker as I'd stuck my head in an auxiliary gym. This man's little girl had also been scheduled to sing hours before. The dad was worried. It was written on his face. The process didn't help him any. There were a couple of gyms where kids waited. Parents weren't allowed in the second gym. Then they went somewhere else in the school that the parents weren't privy to. There's no telling where they actually sang. For all we know, they bussed them to the Simon Cowell's house and back.

Most workers were volunteers. They knew little more about the process besides the directions to the bathroom. I never saw the doting daddy get an answer he wanted. His nervousness planted a seed in me. I began to look for Zac amid the throngs of people.

Peeking in both gyms, a cafeteria, and a hallway, I found him nowhere. I texted him - no answer. Then I checked again in the main gym. While I was looking up into a sea of kids in the bleachers, a man came up to a microphone stand. Into the mic, he made the call for anyone that was scheduled to perform before 2:00 to go into the next gym.

The panic spread quickly. Two o' clock! Zac was scheduled to sing at 11:39. Where was my son?

Fortunately, I calmed down. When I slowed down, evidence mounted that nothing was wrong. Walking back to the cafeteria where the most people seemed to be stacked, I recognized a couple of parents who were there hours ago. I even went back to the van to wait. Within 10 minutes, Zac was finally finished. After he was allowed to turn his phone back on, he returned my text.

The incident reminded me that we can read too much into the circumstances around us. Once emotions flared up, my mind searched for clues that led me to the most-feared conclusion. It wasn't until my reaction settled that I correctly deduced the truth. Jumping to conclusions is a battle we've fought throughout this cancer war. Well-intentioned hearsay, internet rumors, and such receive much more credence when cancer calls. Just like the incident at the all-state chorus try-outs, the panicky father's actions stirred my emotions and led me to the verge of coming unglued. His planted seed also led to an errant conclusion.

Suzette has told me that "life slowed down" after that phone call. It didn't seem like it that first week. Our kids are active, and our schedule is full. The next week was the last week of the grading period. It would be especially busy.

Making out tests and grading papers with a deadline sure wasn't what I felt like doing. With a heavy heart, I did them anyway. So did Suzette. By the next weekend, I was tired and depressed. We still had two weeks to go before we knew Suzette's prognosis. I was certain they would be the longest fourteen days of my life.

I was so very wrong.

Chapter 2

Our family received a blessing. That blessing led to a mindset which has made all the difference in coping with cancer. I wouldn't wish cancer on us or any other family. Yet, God has reversed this negative into a positive. It just took us about a week to realize it.

In the initial week I experienced the extremes – the crying times, the smiling times, and just about every emotion in between. Even when I did find joy, I couldn't let go of the cancer. It was like a somber fog surrounded me. Cancer wasn't always the first thing on my mind, but it was always there. It lingered like a vapor in my brain's crevices and my heart's arteries. Cancer was in her body, but it was dragging me down, too.

On the ninth day after Suzette's cancer diagnosis, the fog lifted. It was a Sunday, and we were at church. Our pastor's chosen scripture and sermon was on Romans 6. On the surface, the verses don't seem to have anything to do with cancer, yet the message hit my heart like Robin Hood's arrow.

Ever since that day, my ears have been open to how God's Word applies to breast cancer. I've been amazed at the hope and direction these verses give. I've come up with a name for verses that give comfort to someone affected by breast cancer. The cross gives comfort and symbolizes hope. A verse, sermon, or devotional that does that in regards to breast cancer I call a "Pink Cross." It's funny. I'd read most of the verses before. Never had they meant so much as they have with this new perspective. Romans 6 became the first Pink Cross.

The more I absorbed our pastor's words, the more I realized that the passage had everything to do with cancer. Verses 11-12 say,

"In the same way, count yourselves dead to sin but alive to God in Christ Jesus. Therefore do not let sin reign in your mortal body so that you obey its evil desires."

I had been doing what the Bible warns us not to do. Miring allowed death and sin to reign over my thoughts and actions. Sure, the diagnosis had been shocking. Of course, I should expect my initial emotions to be extreme. At some point, I had to right myself. I'm reminded of sad songs.

Why is it when someone is down in the dumps and feeling blue they want to hear sad songs? Sad songs do little but depress oneself even more. God doesn't want us to continue in the fog. Verse 11 states, "Count yourself alive to God in Christ Jesus." How can you do that and dwell in depression? Verse 16 continues the thought, "You are slaves to the one whom you obey-whether you are slaves to sin, which leads to death, or to obedience, which leads to righteousness."

I didn't like the cancer prognosis. It drowned my thoughts. After the initial shock, I stayed in the miry pit by choice. Cancer may cast us into the pit, but it can't keep us there. Only we can choose to stay there. In staying there, we choose to be slaves to cancer. It will control our thoughts and actions. I choose not to let cancer win.

No matter what cancer does to my family, it won't win. Jesus has already won the battle over death through salvation on the cross. That thought gives me comfort. Jesus won our battles. Cancer may succeed in the skirmish, but it has no hope of winning the war. Salvation is too strong.

I wasn't the only one who took the sermon to heart.

Our pastor read the scripture. Suzette excused herself to go in the hall. It had made her emotional, she told me later. My bride was gone for ten minutes or more.

At the end of the sermon, she prayed at the altar. A couple of other ladies knelt with her to comfort her. I found when she got back that she had already been comforted. The words, the scripture, the prayer – they all gave Suzette a peace. You could tell it immediately.

Our pastor called her up just before he dismissed the congregation. He laid his hands on her and prayed for her. Some other women came up to her after the sermon wishing her well. It was a scene that could've been sad and tearful. It wasn't. Suzette smiled, accepted all well-wishers, and walked out of the church with her head held high. The power of God had lifted her chin.

Chapter 3

This breast cancer story extends decades before September 20, 2013. In Jasper, Alabama, in 1974 a thirty-eight year old woman died of breast cancer. She left behind a husband and an eight year-old daughter named Suzette.

Martha Miller was a lanky black-haired woman with a thin face and lively smile. She married a Korean War veteran named Hoyt Timmons. They settled in Jasper where Suzette, my future bride, was born.

Martha helped Hoyt run his mobile home business. Little Suzette played in dirt mounds in the lot next to it. Progress cleared those dirt mounds in favor of new businesses and paved lots. Surroundings change. Life did, too, for the Timmons family.

Martha and Hoyt took a trip to Italy. Suzette got a guitar out of the trip. She still has it – an Eko, which I understand is a pretty cool guitar. Suzette's mom returned with something else. A blood test taken when she became sick during the vacation indicated a problem. After returning home, more tests discovered it to be breast cancer.

Over time, Martha's condition worsened, but Suzette didn't know it. The family tried to protect the little girl. Suzette would eventually find out, but it would be on her mother's deathbed. She recalls someone taking her to the hospital to see her mother for one last time.

Shortly after seeing her daughter, Martha Timmons died.

Age thirty-eight is very young to die of cancer. The disease likely robbed Martha Timmons of half her life. Cancer stole a wife away from a husband and a mother away from a young child. The effects lingered for most of Suzette's childhood.

As Suzette became an adult, she was all too aware of the hereditary nature of breast cancer. She scheduled mammograms starting around age thirty. For over a dozen years, the mammograms came back negative. February 2010, the screenings found something. It was a cluster of micro-calcifications in her left breast. A biopsy discovered good news. It was not cancerous. We were relieved, but it was a sign of things to come.

In October of the same year, doctors followed up with an MRI. Something suspicious showed up again in the left breast, leading to another biopsy. It came back benign.

As if seeking equal time, the right breast produced its own suspicious spot on her February 2011 mammogram. A needle biopsy revealed "atypical hyperplasia," rapidly developing abnormal cells. These cells were non-cancerous, but their presence increases a person's risk of developing breast cancer. Doctors surgically removed these abnormal cells. With so much activity in a short amount of time, we expected more spots to start popping up like summer thunderstorms on radar. They didn't. The next two yearly mammograms were clear. That's when the clouds started brewing.

Then came the fall of 2013. The MRI date was September 11. The 9/11 calendar date would now be a red-letter date for a different reason. Like before, something suspicious reared its head on the scan. Doctors ordered a "second-look" ultrasound and a biopsy. This time they found something cancerous. The pathology report blankly states the breast masses are, "strongly Cytokeratin and E-Cadherin positive, consistent with a duct carcinoma." The lady on the phone just called it cancer. The report continued that the largest of the masses consisted of three tumors lined up in a row whose total measurement stretched approximately 5.2 x 3.8 x 2.1 cm...."

The size is scary. Suzette's mammogram a half a year earlier had been clear. Cancerous seeds had been planted in my wife some time in the last six months. The evil had already sprouted and spread, becoming what doctors call "invasive ductal carcinoma." The most significant tumor was close to the chest wall, measuring two and a half centimeters in diameter. It was labeled a "grade 3 tumor," the fastest-growing category. Eventually Suzette's cancer would be classified stage 2-A.

Chapter 4

Hebrews 12:1

"Therefore, since we are surrounded by such a great cloud of witnesses, let us throw off everything that hinders and the sin that so easily entangles, and let us run with perseverance the race marked out for us. Let us fix our eyes upon Jesus."

I had been familiar with this verse before Suzette's cancer diagnosis. Now when I read it, it reflects an even more personal meaning. Hope springs even from the verse's first line. It states, "Therefore, since we are surrounded by such a great cloud of witnesses…"

As teachers, Suzette and I are used to being a center of attention. Since Suzette has developed cancer, we're examined more outside the classroom. It happens whether we like it or not. Friends, family, and acquaintances look for clues to our emotional and physical state. They're inclined to whisper sentences like, "Isn't she the one who has cancer?" or maybe, "She's holding up pretty well." I'm sure it's already happened at most all public places where she's been seen - at church, in the grocery store, at our children's practices. Cancer gives us an audience. We are truly surrounded by a cloud of witnesses.

Suzette didn't want cancer. The reality is that she has it. The audience is there. While we have such a cloud of witnesses, will we be a good witness for Christ? Our witness is more than just what we say to others. It is in how we carry ourselves. What would you do if you knew tomorrow that you would be on stage in front of dozens of people? Would you wear something unique? Would you act crazy? Here's a better question. Will you wear the love of Christ on your sleeve? Would you show God's love through your actions and words? When people look at and listen to you, is it clear that you are a child of God through Jesus Christ?

It's hard to imagine writing this, but it is a fact. A cancer diagnosis is an opportunity. When life gives you lemons, make lemonade. What God can do with cancer is far more profound than a refreshing drink. Being a Christian example in the face of disease, giving God glory for health blessings and new influence, these are the seeds that can appeal to non-believers. Suzette's actions can inspire believers. That inspiration may lead others to plant seeds, too. God is taking advantage of her high-visibility. He is turning this negative into positives.

The next line begins, "Let us throw off everything that hinders and the sin that so easily entangles..." There is no doubt. Cancer is a burden, a monkey on our backs, an endless cloud engulfing us. Cancer is not an easy thing to throw off, but we can. We must. In the first nine days of the cancer diagnosis, I was down and depressed. What good did that depression do? Does it change the fact that Suzette has cancer? Did it do anything to lift her spirits or my family's spirits? No!

Why carry around more burdens than you have to? I have often felt sympathy for those who work in a funeral home. The people who purchase their services are naturally saddened by the loss of their loved one. So what do funeral home workers do? They walk around with the most hangdog, sympathetic expressions on their faces. I'm certainly not condemning them for doing so. It's an expected part of their job. I just am of the mind to do as the Bible says. I want to throw off everything that hinders and entangles. We may not shed the cancer. We can at least shed cancer's emotional burden and put a smile on our faces.

"Let us run with perseverance the race marked out for us." I see children do it all the time – run around like little jackrabbits. Since I am in my forties, quick, unnecessary movement is liable to send me to the hospital. The concept of competing, however, does resonate in me. God has choreographed the course we are to take. It's not a stroll-in-the-park kind of course, either. Life is a knock-down, drag-out battle against sin and the things that hinder us. It's a proverbial race. The metaphor continues.

When you run a race, where are you looking? A competitor stares straight at the finish line. It's the destination.

And it's not just a casual glance. In a race, you are intently fixed upon your goal. This is an "I-want-it" moment. Your purpose in that time span of the race is to get to that destination. Shortly after Suzette was diagnosed with cancer, I had the urge to slow life down. I wanted to resign a committee position in my church. The business of the committee was important and we had a meeting coming up. With Suzette having cancer, it was like those details

23

dropped off the face of the earth. No one would have blamed me if I had let someone else handle those decisions and actions. To make a long story short, I stayed on the committee, and I'm glad.

If I slow down too much, I may look back. When a sprinter runs a race, they don't look back. As a man, I tend to overanalyze everything, including details about cancer. Do sprinters analyze much during a race? Probably only the bad ones do. Introspection can be the devil's workshop. God gives me the direction. My job is to run.

The passage in Hebrews uses the phrase "marked out for us." I am a believer that God works secretly for good in our everyday lives. His actions often go unnoticed or appear insignificant. An example came from a *Sports Illustrated* article by Thomas Lake I read a few years back. It was about a basketball shot made in a Southeastern Conference tournament game in Atlanta. The shooter's name was Mykal Riley of the University of Alabama. Even at face value, the shot held great significance.

Near the end of a game in the SEC tournament, his last-second three-point shot put the game against Mississippi State into overtime. Eight minutes later, just as thousands of fans would have been streaming out of the Georgia Dome, a tornado struck downtown Atlanta. A hole tore in the roof of the Dome, and players ran for cover. No one was injured inside the building. There certainly would have been casualties had Riley made the shot. As the article stated, Riley's feat aptly became known as "The Shot that Saved Lives."

There was more to the story. The article describes the incalculable number of things that had to happen for Mykal

Riley to save all those lives that stormy night in Atlanta. He had quit two colleges and a strange series of circumstances even allowed him to play for the University of Alabama. Moreover, Riley's basketball talent was honed in part because of a horrific crime. Riley's grandmother used an insurance check from the death of his murdered Aunt Ernestine to pay for the basketball court in the yard where he practiced and practiced and practiced his shooting form. That practice enabled him to play college ball and to save all those lives that day with a flick of his wrist.

Deuteronomy 29:29 says, "The secret things belong to the Lord our God." I believe it. The story of Mykal Riley has God's handiwork written all over it.

There is more than just coincidence in our daily lives. The fact that the race is "marked for us," implies that God has predetermined our desired actions. Did God know that Suzette was going to have cancer? Absolutely. What does He want us to do in the race marked for us? He wants us to run it with "perseverance." Perseverance means that we don't give up, that we don't hide in a fog of misery. It is God's plan. It is for His glory.

"Let us fix our eyes upon Jesus." Is there a better way to run the race with perseverance than to keep the love, the example, and the salvation of Jesus as your goal? Like the concentration of a sprinter, we shouldn't just look at Him. He is the focus of our concentration.

As I write this, I am strong. The fog of that first week has lifted. I know challenges to that strength will come. Physical and emotional pain will try to bring back the fog of misery that we had in the first week. Through the encouragement of our family and friends and the hope of

God's word, I pray the fog will be driven away, regardless of the road that lies ahead.

Focusing on Jesus reminds me of a song. It has given me comfort before. The chorus proclaims,

"Turn your eyes upon Jesus,

Look full in His wonderful face,

And the things of earth will grow strangely dim,

In the light of His glory and grace."

Chapter 5

The doctor remained out of town. When we first went to the doctor after the cancer diagnosis, the physician's assistant saw Suzette. We had some decisions to make, but in Suzette's mind, they were already made. She knew early what she wanted and never wavered. Recent breast-cell flares and her mother's cancer had convinced her. She wanted a double mastectomy.

The physician's assistant thought it was a good choice. During subsequent visits to several different health professionals, none have even hinted that cutting off her breasts was a bad call. One of the biggest challenges may be an emotional one.

To say that I'm in tune with women's feelings is laughable. That being said, I can see how a woman would take pride in her breasts. They feed children, attract the opposite sex, and are a symbol of womanhood. I would have understood if Suzette had been reluctant. After all, I had been reluctant to get rid of some of my parts.

Zac was born when Suzette was age thirty-five. I hear that age is kind of a magic number for childbirth. When a baby is born after the mother is thirty-five, there's a bigger chance for pregnancy problems.

In the months before our boy was born, we had ventured into the conversation of which one of us would "get fixed." Honestly, the thoughts of a surgeon messin' with "my boys" threw up red flags in my mind. I didn't say anything, though. Suzette volunteered to have the procedure done while she was in the hospital with Zac, so I guess I was off the hook.

I know I'm comparing nuts to grapefruits. (A-hem) Make that apples to oranges. If I had cancer, I may have felt differently. Either way, Suzette never hesitated in her request for a double mastectomy. "Her girls" were trying to kill her. "The girls" had to go.

The physician's assistant told us more details about the date of the surgery. Before the mastectomy itself, the surgeon would test Suzette's lymph nodes. (The lymph nodes, so it seems, are a pathway to other parts of the body.) We did not want cancer in the lymph nodes.

It turns out that there is far more to having breast cancer than going into one doctor's office, picking a treatment path, and walking into surgery. One of the pleasant surprises of the process is the support. A local non-profit organization called the Cancer Navigators, for example, has a representative that just shows up at our doctor's appointments. We don't pay her, and we never have to remind her. Besides just being there, she informs us about hair loss, insurance companies, and the like. The organization even gave Suzette a pink computer tablet with an app that includes doctor contacts and health references. That's a good service.

Another agency of support is an extension of one of the local hospitals called the Breast Center. In fact, we met with a counselor from the Breast Center before we even saw the surgeon or physician's assistant. In that consultation the BRCA gene mutation test was mentioned – BRCAnalysis it is called. Suzette had already read about it. Someone who tests positive for this gene has a higher risk of breast and ovarian cancer. Plus, it is an inherited gene mutation. If Suzette had tested positive for the gene mutation, each of our sons would have a fifty percent chance of inheriting it. This would have significantly increased their risks for certain types of cancers. This risk could be passed on to their children, too.

The famous actress, Angelina Jolie, had a double mastectomy because she tested positive for the gene mutation. She had reportedly not been diagnosed with cancer but had the surgery as a preventative measure. It is quite a bold move to have your body parts cut off without even a cancer diagnosis. Suzette signed up for the test.

It turns out the BRCAnalysis is more prevalent in the media than out in communities such as ours. Suzette was only the third person in the county to have the testing done locally. Others in the past, if they qualified, had to go through Emory Hospital in Atlanta for the BRCA test. Even then, the waiting list was long, and results didn't come in quickly. Suzette's cancer diagnosis came at the right time, if there is such a thing. Suzette would be qualified, take the tests, and know the results even before the end of the three weeks.

Suzette was less definitive on reconstruction decisions. Surgery would take off her breasts but reconstruction could give her a new pair. The procedure isn't like stitching on a new finger or strapping on a leg prosthesis. Building a new breast requires several doctor visits to fill up the sac implanted inside the chest cavity. We had an appointment with the plastic surgeon. After a short stint in the waiting room, a nurse called us back. She had many questions before we saw the doctor. After taking notes on Suzette's case, the nurse interjected her own commentary. She had great things to say about the doctor, assuring Suzette that "boobies" were his specialty.

The term "booby" is just funnier than the word "breast," just not as socially acceptable. In fact, I hesitate to put too much reference to "boobies" in a book. I have to admit that it is a curious word, probably for all the wrong reasons. The meanings of other "booby" derivations don't have anywhere near the same meaning. I can't imagine the grinning nurse, bragging on how her boss specialized in…say… "a trap intended to surprise a person who unknowingly triggers it." Who does she work for, Crocodile Dundee? There's an even more disjointed meaning of the "b-word" than the trusty "booby trap." There actually is a kind of bird called the "blue-footed booby." I'll try not to imagine what one of those looks like.

Anyway, Suzette opted for reconstructed breasts.

Writing is one of my hobbies. Penning the occasional sports or feature article for my local paper, one could label me a professional writer. That moniker would be misleading. I don't write as often as a real professional writer would. The craft gives me entertainment and a small source of income. It serves other purposes, too. Writing helped me cope with the death of my father in 2006. It was no surprise when I started penning this manuscript about breast cancer shortly after Suzette's diagnosis. As I continued punching the keys in those days after diagnosis, I realized something. A book about breast cancer can be more than just therapy. Oddly enough, a bathroom urge led me to one other reason.

I was in the restroom in Arby's. There I spied something completely unexpected. It was a poem. The single sheet hung up in a frame on the far wall. With my curiosity piqued, I moved in closer. It was Robert Frost's, "The Road Not Taken." I was already familiar with the poem, but I read on anyway. It made me think.

"Two roads diverged in a yellow wood,

And sorry I could not travel both

And be one traveler, long I stood

And looked down one as far as I could

To where it bent in the undergrowth;

Then took the other, as just as fair,

And having perhaps the better claim

Because it was grassy and wanted wear,

Though as for that the passing there

Had worn them really about the same,

And both that morning equally lay

In leaves no step had trodden black.

Oh, I kept the first for another day!

Yet knowing how way leads on to way

I doubted if I should ever come back.

I shall be telling this with a sigh

Somewhere ages and ages hence:

Two roads diverged in a wood, and I,

I took the one less traveled by,

And that has made all the difference."

On the road of life, people like to know what's coming. Comfort comes with knowledge. It's why most take the well-worn path. Most references to Frost's poem endorse choosing the road not taken. Not this reference. Cancer chose our particular path.

Like Frost's traveler, others will follow our path. As I browsed the poem in the bathroom of a roast beef joint, I made the connection. Others might want to read this manuscript. They wouldn't read for any expertise in breast cancer or the psychology of having a disease. I'm just learning about the disease myself. I'm just a man whose family is traveling down a new path, recording what inspires me along the way. For those who find themselves taking the same path, I hope this presents a refreshing Christian perspective...and maybe even some comfort.

There are other reasons to write. Finances are secondary to Suzette's health, but I'd be oblivious to think that medical bills will not mount quickly. We will owe more money than I care to think about. By chronicling and publishing our journey, any proceeds made are at least a step toward the inevitable debt to come.

Furthermore, this publication provides an avenue for well-wishers. Through phone calls, texts, and social media, our family, church, and co-workers know of Suzette's cancer.

Many have already reached out to express sympathy and concern. Numerous friends, family, and acquaintances genuinely want to help us. Several have asked, "What I can do to help?" I would graciously accept their help. It's just that no practical avenue of their generosity comes to mind when they ask. The conversation inevitably ends with an undesired result. The willing helpers end the conversation without helping. The gracious receivers of help end the conversation without getting help. The cycle happens all the time. With this book, maybe it can end. Friends, this is how you can help. Buy the book. Profit from it will help us out.

Chapter 6

The other night, I was reading in 1 Samuel. A passage struck me about God's attitude toward mourning. Chapter 16 begins.

The Lord said to Samuel,

"How long will you mourn for Saul, since I have rejected him as king over Israel? Fill your horn with oil and be on your way."

This isn't the Saul that changed his name to Paul in the New Testament. He was an ancient ruler of Israel. Samuel had been the previous God-appointed ruler of the land. In his old age, Saul took over. Despite Samuel's tutelage, Saul's reign was ineffective. The pupil fell out of God's favor. That's when God spoke to Samuel. I know a little bit how the old prophet felt. A teacher holds hope for his student's success. When Saul was on the downslide, Samuel mourned. To use my analogy, Samuel was in a fog. So, what does God tell Samuel in his time of mourning? He says, "Fill your horn with oil and be on your way."

In other words, "Get over it!"

"Getting over it" is easier said than done when cancer calls. At some point after the shock of the diagnosis, life must go on. It's not just a cliché. It's what God wants.

We parents often give direction without a purpose. It's not a fault of ours. We just don't have God's omnipotence. When we tell our kids it's too warm to wear a coat, we don't know that the classroom's air conditioning might be unbearably cold. We may persuade our reluctant son to play football, only to have him get hurt.

God's directives have more foresight, and this scripture is a perfect example. Samuel was not only to be on his way. He was to fill his horn with oil. Later in the chapter, Samuel would use that oil to anoint a future king. That king, David, would have a far wider reach and impact than Saul.

God has a plan for the future. Certainly, today's disappointments may seem overwhelming. We can't let the burden of mourning linger around us like a fog. Let's take God's advice, "Get over it." It's a command laced with compassion. The Bible reassures us that He holds the future.

Don't let life's obstacles strangle you. God holds you in His hand. Trust Him.

The same sentiment and comfort is found in Philippians 4:6-7. It says,

"Do not be anxious about anything but in everything, by prayer and petition, with thanksgiving, present your requests to God. And the peace of God, which transcends all understanding, will guard your hearts and your minds in Christ Jesus."

Don't hold on to those burdens of cancer. In presenting your requests to God, be willing to let Him lift that burden. I know it's hard. Having read part of our cancer story, you know that we've struggled, too. Yet, we know to surrender our burdens to God. If you do so, the "peace of God, will guard your hearts and your minds in Christ Jesus."

Chapter 7

I went to a wedding not long ago. The groom was a friend of mine. Suzette and I wed nearly twenty years ago. I cannot begin to count the number of weddings I've attended since. Seems like every one makes me think about my own wedding. At this one, I hadn't thought much about mine until the wedding veered from the script.

The mistakes and ad libs began when the pastor said to the groom, "Repeat after me." Maybe he was overzealous or just nervous. The pastor then stated a long sentence for my friend to repeat. By the time the groom spoke, he'd forgotten what he was supposed to say. To use a football analogy, the preacher had to drop back and punt. Starting over, the pastor then messed up the lines. After an extended laugh, the minister finally got it right, but the wedding wasn't the same. The bride and groom accepted the faux pas as a license to ad lib. The mistakes reminded me even more about December 18, 1993. I can recall it like it was yesterday.

Our first wedding mistake happened before the preacher even spoke. A quick decision, made moments before I took my place beside the preacher, doomed it to happen. The person recording the wedding video decided to put a microphone on me. The problem – Suzette didn't know about the mic.

The big moment arrived. The pianist played "Here Comes the Bride." Suzette in all her beauty walked slowly down the aisle, her father at her arm. From the front of the church, I spied a crimson tint to her neck. When Suzette gets nervous, her skin from her upper chest to her chin becomes red. Her anxiety must have led to her being chatty. When Suzette met me on the stage in front of everyone, she held my hand and completed a thought by saying, "Something to hold on to." I knew the microphone had picked it up. Just as she started, I shushed her.

The first thing you say to your wife, especially on her wedding day, should be gentle and loving. Since Suzette abided by the tradition of not seeing (or speaking with) the groom on her wedding day, the first thing I said to my wife was neither gentle nor loving. "Ssshhhhhhhhhhh!" I quickly blurted in response to her comment.

For whatever reason, Suzette didn't hold that mistake against me. A woman who gets shushed on her wedding day probably has the right to be ill. Anyway, the mistakes continued.

Suzette's cousin is a preacher. He performed the ceremony. He's not short. He's just not as tall as either Suzette or me. Once Suzette walked down the aisle, we met on stage and turned toward the preacher. I saw it on the video. It was like an eclipse. He completely disappeared to all the sanctuary. A faceless, muffled voice conducted the ceremony. I don't know if it ruffled him or not. If it did, that might explain the next wedding deviation.

When he gave me the ring to put on her finger, it was the wrong ring. The audience probably never noticed me hand it back. He figured out his mistake quickly enough, but our ring problems weren't over yet.

Words were spoken and repeated while I placed the ring on Suzette's finger. At least I tried to place it on her finger. I couldn't get it past her knuckle. While I frantically pushed, Suzette's cousin thoughtfully explained the holy significance of a ring's circular nature - the representation of Christ's never-ending love.

It was a passage I'd requested we include in the ceremony. I'd heard it at a wedding years before and liked it. A month or two before our wedding, I'd even phoned the pastor who'd conducted that particular ceremony to get the exact wordage.

Standing in front of family and friends, we came to my requested part, but I barely heard it. I spent my energy trying to get Suzette's ring past her knuckle. Just as he finished speaking that part, the ring finally found its lifetime home fully in place.

After the "I do's" and the kiss, the missteps kept coming, literally in one case. We were pronounced man and wife. I stepped off the stage in my slick-bottomed, brand-new shoes and slipped on the carpeted step! Fortunately, my footing stabilized enough to keep me from really making a fool of myself.

I could say that the blunders ceased with the end of the ceremony. That, of course would be a horribly very false statement.

We were booked at Edgewater Resorts in Panama City Beach, Florida, (Room 706, to be precise). If someone attending our 2:00 pm wedding had wanted to make the drive, they could've heard the crash of the waves by bedtime. We wouldn't hear them until shortly before 4:00 am. Here's why.

Our first mistake was hiring the slowest camerawoman known to mankind. While our friends and family partook of wedding cake and hors d' oeuvres, the camerawoman took us back into the sanctuary for a marathon of snail-paced shots. Those waiting to see us must've been bored out of their gourds by the time we finished.

There was one productive group during that time, however. The men not in the wedding party pictures took it upon themselves to decorate my car. Our slow camerawoman gave them plenty of time for the task. Those fellows must've spent all their money on shaving cream that day. It was everywhere both inside and outside the car. I don't know what brand they used, but what they put on the windshield of my Camaro stuck like magnets on a refrigerator. We stopped two or three times in the first twenty-five miles of our honeymoon trip, just trying to clean that mess off. It was near dark before we finally got an hour out of Jasper.

To round out the trip, I got lost on the way to the beach. We must have driven sixty or more miles out of the way before we finally parked under a Florida palm tree, staggered into Edgewater, and claimed our reservation.

The wedding had its share of mistakes, but the marriage was definitely not a mistake. We've been a very happy couple for nearly twenty years.

There's a picture on Suzette's dresser. It was taken on our ten-year anniversary trip. It caught my eye the other day. It's a shot of Suzette and me on our first cruise. I remember the picture circumstances well. (Those of you who have taken a cruise know that ship cameramen are everywhere, snapping pictures.) We were in the dining room when I spied the cameraman making his way down the row. He took pictures of any willing family or group seated at the tables preceding ours. When he came to us, I was prepared. As the man lifted his camera toward his face to prepare a shot, I reached beside Suzette's neck with my left hand, put my right arm over her shoulder, and surprised her with a kiss. The camera snapped the shot in mid-smooch. Suzette's surprised expression was captured and has been on display on her dresser ever since.

The memory of that kiss makes me smile and think about kisses.

Since cancer entered our world, our kisses have been longer. Our hugs have been stronger. Life doesn't slow down, but when I'm close to my wife, the importance of a good embrace keeps me close.

The perks of life are harder to resist now. If Suzette wants to eat out, I don't have as much heart to resist. Not long ago, Suzette told me that she wanted a breast cancer bracelet, something she could add a bead to for each month she's cancer-free. I didn't even ask about its cost. I like the thought of a "cancer-free" future. My head instinctively nodded in approval of the purchase.

Suzette did make a curious purchase the other day. We were shopping at Ross. She pulled off the rack a pair of jeans. In the twenty-plus years I've known her, I never have seen her in a pair of these. The jeans had sequins on the back pockets. Before you all yawn at once, let me set this up. Suzette is a very conservative dresser. She's not one to excessively expose her thigh and mid-riff, and hints of cleavage are usually non-existent.

Despite my mildly surprised look, she bought those jeans. Now my ultra-conservative wife will walk around with flashy things on her booty. She joked, "If you no longer have some body parts, you have to accentuate others."

Since the purchase, her modesty has re-emerged. She has yet to don that pair of jeans. I wonder if she ever will.

Chapter 8

It was a Sunday morning. I was watching Marvin Cherry of the Hightown Church of God preach on TV. Once again the Bible's message spoke to me within the context of breast cancer. I can't recall exactly what verses Cherry quoted, but they contrasted God's will to the ever-changing ways of the world. The point is that what we see is subject to change. There is hope in what's subject to change.

There's nothing quite like an eloquent preacher. When the right message is delivered the right way, it's hard not to take notice. The scripture Cherry quoted coupled with that of another pastor's sermon. The two combined with my interpretations to make another pink cross.

The preacher resounded, "If you don't have a job, it's subject to change. If you are broke, it's subject to change. If you have breast cancer, it's subject to change." The cancer reference would normally have gotten my attention, but he already had it. The message hit home. Things of this world will change, even things that appear permanent. What's not subject to change is God. We should spend our time, energy, and love on things that have to do with God. We must have patience with the burdens of the world. Cherry pointed out that God blesses the ones He loves and that

God works to make things good, "Don't throw in the towel. It's subject to change. Don't let the devil run you away. It's subject to change."

The point is to live by faith and not by sight. I'm reminded of the old song.

> "Standing on the promises of Christ my King,
>
> Through eternal ages let his praises ring;
>
> Glory in the highest, I will shout and sing,
>
> Standing on the promises of God.
>
> Standing, standing,
>
> Standing on the promises of Christ my Savior;
>
> Standing, standing,
>
> I'm standing on the promises of God."

That particular sermon inevitably ended, and I ended up on a different channel. The message from Gardendale Baptist Church also inspired me. Their senior pastor is Kevin Hamm. He quoted Isaiah 43: 18-19, 21.

God spoke to the Israelites.

"Forget the former things; do not dwell on the past. See, I am doing a new thing! Now it springs up; do you not perceive it?...I provide water in the wilderness and streams in the wasteland, to give drink to my people, my chosen, the people I formed for myself that they may proclaim my praise."

The verse caught my attention. What a simple command – "Forget the former things." I realize that's not an easy task. God clarifies, "Do not dwell on the past." I get the sense that the word "dwelling" means more than just a recollection of past times. The verb "dwell" is synonymous with the word "reside." Do not reside in the past. God wants us to go forward, to live more for the present and the future rather than the past.

In verse 19, we're reminded of the difference between our perspective and God's perspective. He states, "I am doing a new thing...Do you not perceive it?"

God's work isn't always understood. The Israelites did not perceive it well either. God works past our perspective, and His work is for our good. I think the Gardendale pastor said it appropriately. "He is weaving your storms for His glory." God orchestrates successes from our crises. Our faith reminds us that God is all-powerful. That faith is especially important in a crisis when our perspectives are even narrower.

Satan is quick to act in times of crisis when we are willing to listen to anything. In giving too much credence to casual doctor comment or friend hearsay, we leave the door open to fear and worry. Cancer and crisis are a breeding ground for Satan. Don't give up. Don't let the enemy win. Let God win. God has His hand in every life every day. Storms and crises seem big, but they are not as big as we've made them out to be. Jesus has already won the war. Don't let cancer come along and steal one bit of His glory. What the enemy uses to break you, let God use to bless you.

I'm sure parents can identify. The word "no" is a child's least favorite answer. We say it all the time. To which comes the inevitable response, "Why?"

Sometimes that is a very hard question to answer. Our judgment alone should qualify as a good answer. That doesn't satisfy the persistent child. So how are we inclined to answer the "why" question? To a child, it's an even less satisfactory response, "Because I said so!"

God doesn't do that. Verse 21 gives purpose to God's command. Just like children, we accept more with a reason. And how can we argue with God's reasoning: "that they may proclaim my praise"? How we react to cancer can be our biggest witness for God's glory.

Someone's witness, the way she carry herself in Christ, is often more of an influence than written or spoken words. The Bible references silent influence and how it compares to a town. Matthew 5:14-16 states, "You are the light of the world. A town built on a hill cannot be hidden. Neither do people light a lamp and put it under a bowl. Instead they put it on its stand, and it gives light to everyone in the house. In the same way, let your light shine before others, that they may see your good deeds and glorify your Father in Heaven."

To experience crisis through the will and the peace of God is quite admirable. It's a valuable tool to attract those who are lost in this world. When life throws your family the cancer curveball, don't duck and run. Stand and take your best swing. Whether you hit a home run or strike out, your actions make it easier for others to step into the batter's box and face cancer. Have no fear in facing cancer, for you are not alone. Isaiah 41:10 reminds us, "So do not fear, for I am with you; do not be dismayed, for I am your God. I will strengthen you and help you; I will uphold you with my righteous right hand.

Chapter 9

It's one thing to say that an attitude about cancer has changed. It's another thing to show it. Cancer doesn't keep Suzette from enjoying life. A visit to the doctor recently reminded me of that fact.

Suzette and I had been in the waiting room forever. The doctor's office was nearly an hour slow. A nurse actually came out and offered complimentary bottles of water and packs of crackers to satisfy the restless. Finally, we were called back, which just meant that our wait continued in a different room. It was the examination room where the doctor would see Suzette. At least we were the only ones in there.

I don't know if the music had been playing in the other room or not. Maybe this smaller room allowed us to hear it more plainly. We paid only casual attention to it at first. Then came a song by a duo which I had neither heard nor thought about in ages.

"Love, Love will keep us together

Think of me babe whenever"

It was Captain and Tennille's "Love Will Keep us Together." I kind of liked the old pop pair, but not as much as Suzette did. She quickly started singing along to the lyrics.

"Some sweet talkin' girl comes along singin' his song

Don't mess around,

You just got to be strong"

(I added a crude dance move, shaking my shoulders to the beat, moving my hands, too.)

"Just stop, 'cause I really love You

Stop, I'll be thinking of you

Look in my heart and let love keep us together"

We must have been quite a sight. Later I thought, "How many freshly diagnosed cancer patients are having so much fun?" That's my wife. She's busy living, not busy dying.

Suzette's social media posts also reflect that attitude. Not long ago, she used a Facebook post to ask a curious question. She wrote,

"Ok. Time to be creative. I need a NAME for my tumor....tired of saying 'the tumor this...the cancer that'. I found out more about 'him' today...sorry guys, it has to be a him...you'll see why. 'He' was about an inch in size....not huge, but certainly not small either....'He' was classified as grade 3 - the fastest growing of his kind. 'He' is ER and PR positive, which means 'he' likes female hormones and has little receptors on the outside with which to grab them. 'He' fashioned himself as quite the 'lady killer'-- pun intended…So, what shall we call him? Taking suggestions now."

I love her personality, and Suzette isn't letting cancer consume it. It would've been easy to rouse sympathy by throwing her hands up in the air, proclaiming her doom and gloom on social media. She didn't. Doing that doesn't help her go forward, and it's probably not what God wants others to do, either.

Even though we have a peace about her cancer, I certainly have a sense of anticipation about the post-surgery conference with her doctor. That's when we'll know if cancer has spread to the lymph nodes. It will tell us whether radiation is required. The doctor will have seen the tumor and can give us a prognosis.

I have imagined the scene many times. The first part of the discussion has no variables, regardless of Suzette's prognosis.

First, I will be summoned to a small room in the bowels of the hospital. The doctor will come in and shake my hand. "Mr. Mitchell," he will say.

From then on, I imagine I might hear any phrase from "cancer-free" to "there is a problem." For some strange reason, my thoughts of this conversation with the doctor lead me to think about the game show, *Family Feud*.

Earlier I mentioned how we tend to ignore reality by hearing what we want to hear. Even if the doctor says dire things about the surgery and prognosis, our coping mechanisms may interpret it to be less severe. A similar phenomenon used to happen on the Feud.

Family members are somehow convinced that their idiot cousin's answer is a good answer. The host walks all the way down to the end of the table. That's where the family always sticks the idiot cousin. The host leans on the desk, forcing his eye off the family's cute blonde niece just long enough to read the question. He says, "Name something you might buy at a movie theatre."

Idiot cousin stands with a blank stare. The audience can tell his wheels are turning. They're going pretty slow, but they are turning. All the obvious answers like "popcorn" and "candy" being used up aren't helping his decision. Finally, he says with misguided confidence, "milk."

The live studio audience rolls their eyes collectively. They know there's a better chance of William Shatner joining One Direction than of that answer flipping over on the big board. Somehow the family is blind to logic. Every one of them instantaneously convince themselves that "milk" is not only an appropriate response, but one of the highest quality.

"Good answer! Good answer! Milk! Show me milk! Good answer!"

Then the buzzer sounds, signifying the missed answer. The family gives an "awwww," like they were actually surprised. It apparently was a huge shock to them that not even one of the 100 audience members polled thought that milk and Goobers weren't part of some movie theatre value package.

When the doctor shakes my hand and begins to speak on the 11th after surgery, no matter what I hear, my mind might spin it into a comfortable answer.

"Stage 4? We need radiation now? Yes! Radiation! I agree, Doc. That's a good answer! A good answer!"

I'm not really dreading that conversation too much. The farther along these two weeks go, the less I worry about what the doctor will say. I don't worry much about the prognosis. God has put a comfort in my heart. When I spin an answer into what I want, I'm refusing to allow change. If I read the Bible correctly, God doesn't encourage us to dwell much in the past.

I just hope the doctor doesn't confuse me with another family member so that I agree to something that doesn't even apply to Suzette. "Mr. Mitchell, we'll have to amputate the other ear and take part of her nose off. Will you sign the papers?"

I can see myself with a glazed, stupid-cousin look, finally saying, "Ear? Need to cut it off now? Yes! Amputation! Good answer, Doc! Good answer!"

The weekend before the surgery, we went to an Alabama home football game. My wife and I both went to school there. The band, the campus atmosphere, and the trip itself made it an enjoyable experience - even for a non-football fan such as Suzette.

I didn't notice her at first. About three rows in front of us sat one of the feeblest maturing ladies I had ever seen. If she weighed ninety pounds, my name is Justin Bieber. Her arms couldn't have been much wider than pool sticks. Instantly, I felt sad for her. I thought, "Could she have cancer? Her body looked like it. Her hair was a little thin, but I couldn't tell for sure if it was chemo-induced thin or just old-age thin. For a moment, I thought, "What if Suzette looks like this someday?" For an instant, I felt pity not only for her but for what Suzette might become.

Then she looked to the side, and I saw her face. I had expected a feeble, pitiful countenance to match her frail body. Surely someone in that bad a shape wouldn't have any reason to smile. I was trying to read the book by its cover. You know how that turns out. The frail old lady didn't have that look. Across her face was a genuine smile. If something was physically ailing her, she didn't show it. God doesn't want cancer or any other disease to immobilize us.

My children both like acting. One or both frequently perform in the community theater. The stage is not like real life. On the stage, a character may not change. He must exhibit the same traits and emotional demeanor the entire time on stage. Life is more complex, yet sometimes people get caught up in how they are supposed to act. Just because sadness and anger immediately fill our brains following a cancer diagnosis, this doesn't mean they have to stay there. Events beyond our control may start the emotional cycle, but our attitude ends it. In other words, people generally choose their long-term emotions.

I can't pretend to know anything about that feeble little lady at the game. My casual look at her face gave me a spark of inspiration that life has a lot to do with what we make it, not what our circumstances make it.

I'm not the only one with this opinion. God has given Suzette a great peace about cancer and surgery. Even in the first week, she showed great resilience around the children and in general. It turned around that Sunday. In the weeks since, I don't think I saw Suzette cry even once. It has reflected in our children, too.

Our school counselor wanted to check on Zac a couple of days before the surgery. She called him in to her office to talk. I was impressed by what happened. The counselor later sent an e-mail out to Suzette and me later that day. It read, "Zac has an amazingly healthy balance in his understanding of the surgery and aftercare. He is sooo perceptive, as you know! His faith is a strong and positive support for him and you. He is doing well, I believe. He volunteered to come and give me an update every week or so."

Boys tend to handcuff themselves emotionally. It is part of the chromosomal balance. Seeing the report from the counselor gave me comfort about Zac.

With the possible body deterioration cancer and its treatment may bring, it'll be hard enough for the kids to stay strong. For the most part, they look to us for our emotional example in new events. If we are strong in the face of cancer, they will be, too. There is one thing that I've let slide after the cancer diagnosis.

The waiter sat the burrito down in front of me. Cheese sauce covered the meal like the media covered the Super Bowl. It was our first meal after Suzette found out that she had cancer. I quickly picked up my fork and cut. The pulled pork inside the tortilla stuck out like a tan man in a white tux. I balanced the extracted piece on my fork, bringing it up toward my mouth. Nothing would've tasted good after a cancer diagnosis. I chose the burrito anyway. In downing that pork, tortilla cheese, sweetened tea, I broke my diet. Stretching back to March, I had effectively stuck to a diet for just over six months, losing sixty-three pounds in the process.

For a half a year, I had full-fledged tackled my weight problem. With that meal, I reversed course, proceeding headlong back toward obesity. With the diet on hold, I gained back twelve pounds in the first ten days. After a month, I was up twenty pounds.

It's ironic. Suzette's diagnosis prompted her to go on a diet. It got me off mine. Sensing the probability of future chemo, she decided to make herself healthier. She bought corn, beans, okra, salad, and other vegetables. Through the surgery, she stuck to her regimen.

Shortly after a week, we started feeling peace about the diagnosis. I found it hard to get back on the diet wagon even then. About the time I got back in the frame of mind to diet, a Southern phenomenon put food in my face.

Co-workers, friends, Suzette's Sunday school class – they started bringing food. Let me scratch the tip of the iceberg. Our refrigerator filled quickly with the likes of Honey-Baked Ham, pot roast, chicken casserole, macaroni and cheese, baked potatoes, lasagna, and taco soup. That wasn't all. Some of the desserts included carrot cake cupcakes, cheesecake, and chocolate pound cake.

I deeply appreciated every finger that prepared the meals. I drowned in deliciousness the entire time, consuming far more than my share of all that food. Suzette ate, but rarely did our boys. With a sixteen and twelve year-old, one would think that they'd have been quick to partake in the rounds of meals that just arrived periodically at our door.

No.

Somewhere in the raising of our children we went wrong when it came to eating. For whatever reasons, both Alex and Zac are picky eaters. About the only staples of their eating desires are chicken fingers, quesadillas, and dessert. Everything else, they either won't try or they like for a fleeting meal or two, just long enough for us to buy a bunch of that food and let it side untouched in our cabinet or fridge. We've noticed the irony before when we eat covered-dish meals at church. With all those fine cooks bringing their best, Suzette and I find ourselves not having enough stomach room to hold all that we want. Even on a diet, there's plenty I can eat. When we get to the table, our plates piled high, we notice the boys' food choices. They might have a couple of Ritz crackers or a roll. The battle begins soon after when we fend off the "can we have dessert" questions.

The boys turned up their noses at almost every single non-dessert brought to our house in that span. There I was with all that food keeping me company. The diet would have to wait.

Chapter 10

The kids' fear of good food probably comes from me. In my childhood, I remember having a boat-load of fear. Some of it was about eating new foods. Other fears were not. Ah! I remember well the fears of youth - the proverbial monster under my bed, my mother forgetting to pick me up, even no one wanting to play with me at school. I lost all those fears when I got older. Now I deal with the fears of adulthood – loneliness, finances, cancer. We got over the monster under our bed and all the childhood fears. Can we get over the grown-up ones? What does the Bible say?

The Bible says many things about fear. It acknowledges it, but it insists that there is no need to fear. Psalm 23:4 – "Even though I walk through the valley of the shadow of death, I will fear no evil, for You are with me."

Isaiah 41:10 reads, "So do not fear, for I am with you; do not be dismayed, for I am your God. I will strengthen you and help you."

Psalm 27:1 continues, "The Lord is my light and my salvation-- whom shall I fear? The Lord is the stronghold of my life-- of whom shall I be afraid?"

Psalm 118:6 states, "The LORD is with me; I will not be afraid. What can man do to me?"

Deuteronomy 31:6 says, "Be strong and courageous. Do not be afraid or terrified because of them, for the LORD your God goes with you; He will never leave you nor forsake you."

If fear is the disease, then God is the cure. The promise of salvation has trumped death. Dying and fears that go with it lose their sting. The Bible seems clear. Embrace God, and the fears of the world will not be as strong.

It reminds me of the lyrics to the U2 song, "Kite." It goes like this.

"I'm not afraid to die

I'm not afraid to live

And when I'm flat on my back

I hope to feel like I did"

Our faith gives us comfort. If we can truly say, "I'm not afraid to die. I'm not afraid to live," we will have no fear. When a cancer diagnosis floors you, get up and fight. Don't look back. Go headlong into life, not headlong into death. There are some more lines of the song that I like.

"Who's to say where the wind will take you?

Who's to say what it is will break you?

I don't know, which way the wind will blow"

I like control, but often things work out best when I let go. That hurt me some back when I coached basketball.

I knew the game pretty well and had a small measure of success. One of my weaknesses was the control factor. I found myself having the desire to dictate and choreograph near every move on the court. With a motion offense, I could design where every player would be on the offensive end. We even had scripted lanes to run in going down the court to the other end. In retrospect, our offensive plays probably limited one of the most precious qualities of athletes – the ability to react. Literally, I was doing all the thinking for them. I remember one of my first teams. When ball went out of bounds under our goal, all five players would look to me for the play. They were dependent on me.

Most of the time I could give a good guess at the game's upcoming actions, but the fact is that a basketball game is not a script. It is a series of actions and reactions. Reactions can be predictable only to a degree. Unpredictability isn't the norm in every game, but it is there. In any scripted play, nobody knows exactly how defenders would react. To use the analogy of the song, I truly didn't know which way the wind would blow.

Chapter 11

I've known it all along, but it took cancer in my family to truly realize it. Everyone needs a support system. Husbands, wives, family, friends, church families, and coworkers are like soft pillows in what can be a rocky world. When the world is especially sharp and unforgiving, you need support the most. I can only imagine how emotionally taxing a cancer diagnosis would be without someone to hold, someone to talk to, someone to pray for you.

Our family lives in a hay field a little over twenty miles from our school. The church we attend sits close to fifteen miles in the other direction. Living in Alabama and working in Georgia leaves us out of touch with the people in both states. In the past, Suzette has lamented that we don't have any close friends. Having cancer has changed that outlook.

The days after the revelation of cancer were filled with an outpouring of support. She got calls, texts, and messages. She put her diagnosis on social media. This generated an influx of comments, all wishing her well. Many lifted prayers for her. Our total messages and cards haven't rivaled that of Santa, but the sentiments have struck a chord with Suzette. You may have already connected this analogy. It reminds me of the character George Bailey in *It's a Wonderful Life*.

In a crisis George realized just how many friends he had. The bustle of daily life blinded him from that truth. I can see the scene now. The wind picked up at the cemetery. George had just seen his brother Harry's grave and headstone. He had fallen through the ice because George had not been there to save him. In a moment of revelation, Clarence reminded him, "You see, George. You really did have a wonderful life."

We have felt a little like the Baileys in the final scene where friend after friend came to their house and gave them money. What was it the angel, Clarence, had signed in the book the Bailey's found under the Christmas tree? I believe it read, "No man is a failure who has friends." Sometimes even Hollywood wisdom is right on the money. Even our family, who lives most of our lives under a shell, has found more friends than we ever thought we had.

Suzette entered surgery with a comfort that her name was on the hearts of many, not just on the hearts of few. A warm-hearted surprise came from Suzette's students. She teaches eleven to fourteen-year-old students. At that immature age, few students can be considered mature. The immaturity often takes on two forms.

Some kids are like velcro. They can become attached and are a little bit needy. They want to know the teacher's opinions on everything, and they want to know everything about you. These students become your third hip. It's not bad to be someone's third hip. You realize though, that the attachment is based more on them than it is you. The velcro works on other adults, too. They stick to most anyone – crosswalk workers, the lady at the Wal-Mart register, or the guy behind the counter at the pharmacy. They probably have a stuffed frog or bear at home that they cling to once they get home because they now have no more adults to cling to.

Then there is the other extreme. The students are too cool for school. They put up their walls to all adults. This group has perfected the art of "the shun." The first adult in their daily path is their teacher. Those who are highly practiced in the Zen art of "shunnism" have no problem talking to their teacher – under certain circumstances, of course. If you call on them in class, they'll answer, provided what they say that makes them look cool. Sometimes there is another purpose. They may prefer to distribute a wrong answer. That sometimes gives them a stage in which to perpetuate their image. I'll use the girls as an example first. The bad girl will say, "Man, I would tell Monet dude that if you're going to paint nature, you need to show the frog guts and stuff."

The ditzy blonde will say, "Oh, I don't like Monet. He doesn't paint things like hot guys. If he did that, I'd get my Daddy to buy his paintings."

The true beauty will steer clear of answering, especially if she is on the front row. Her energy goes into looking beautiful. She'll just rotate her neck on a swivel, revolving her hair around in a big cascade. These girls are like a waterfall in a hotel lobby. They catch everybody's eye. Swiveling her head isn't all they do. The beauty might bat her eyelashes and look bashful all the time. Consequently, she may not have to do much the whole year, and it will have nothing to do with the teacher. All she has to do is to give a sweet and innocent look at some helpless guy around her, and, before you know it, he's offering to sharpen her pencil, give her a sheet of paper, and do her homework for her.

The guys are less subtle. You can tell what they're thinking from a mile away. Some are bashful. They daydream of talking to that girl who sits up front. The odds of that happening are close that of man going to Mars in a Volkswagen bus. These kids might actually talk to you in private, but them speaking in front of the class can be a big deal. It's ironic. Speaking to the group is probably their only chance to impress the people in the social cliques that they can't get into. They're too afraid what they say will be some window to the soul that they don't want opened. They don't want others to come in.

Your future car salesmen, politicians, and comedians have figured out that they can mask who they really are. That knowledge gives them the license to be completely extroverted. With these students, they are truly liable to say anything. One of them might interject something like, "Monet sucks like my mom's vacuum cleaner."

Growing up is such a self-conscious phase. The people around them are distant planets to their center of their universe. While we expected our family and friends to have a true, heartfelt reaction to Suzette's cancer diagnosis, we didn't expect the same out of many students. We were wrong.

The first poster says, "We love you!" right across the middle in red letters. Around it are signatures of twenty or more seventh grade students. With some of the names were personalized messages like, "Stay strong! We're thinking about you," or "Keep fighting, Mrs. Mitchell!" Suzette had it taped on the wall beside our bed for the longest of times. Even now that it's on a dresser, it's one of the first things she sees when she wakes up each morning.

Her sixth graders did the same thing. One student came up with an idea and got it passed around in their homeroom class for others to sign it. The words were in purple in the center, but all the signatures were in pink ink.

Suzette's eighth graders were even more personal. A couple of them bought her a little, pink bear. Another girl crocheted her a pink hat with a ribbon on it. The boys surprised her, too. Two days before the surgery, four guys in her class wore pink just for her. A couple of these guys were some of the best athletes in school. They disregarded their tough-guy reputation to show support for their sick math teacher. That meant a lot. With that very class, near the end of Suzette's last day before surgery, one girl wanted to hug her. Another standing nearby wanted the same. Before Suzette knew it, the entire class was in a group-hug. Someone took a picture and sent it to Suzette while she was being prepped for the operation the next day. There was another day in recent memory when she needed a hug. At the time it had nothing to do with cancer.

We'd heard the weather would be bad. Meteorologists began warning the South about a high probability of killer tornadoes forming over the region a few days ahead of time. There was nothing subtle about it. Bad weather was on the way for April 27, 2011.

The couple of days beforehand held a strange feeling. The South is no stranger to storm systems. This forecast covered a wide area and predicted a high degree of ferocity. Many people were scared. All the internet prognoses showed a large bubble of red covering almost the entire state. This was the area where dangerous tornadoes were most likely to occur. We all went on with our lives, keeping an eye toward the weather that day, April 27, 2011.

It came with a vengeance. We wouldn't have to wait long on the action to reach our area. In western sections of our state, the first wave hit the ground near the middle of the night. It was a thin line of precipitation whose power lay not in the rain, but in the wind that it brought. It reached our area during our school's 1st period.

At Zac's elementary school, it dropped a mammoth tree. It missed the school but took out the tops of a few hapless cars. The power went out at our school and stayed out for the rest of the day. We'd heard reports of damage in town. A lady who lived a few miles down the road lost her house completely. A falling tree targeted it, collapsing a bedroom, just moments after her son had awakened and walked to another part of the house. This first wave was in and out of the area quickly, but this was not all. The main storms would come that evening.

If you aren't from the area, you may not know. That fateful day lives in infamy across a large portion of the Southeast. The National Weather Service said that that day "will go down as one of the most historic and severe weather outbreaks in United States history." The state of Alabama alone suffered through sixty-two tornados. Since 1874, in Alabama only six EF-5 tornados have been recorded. Three of them were registered on April 27th alone. According to the National Weather Service, the storms accounted for 247 deaths across the state of Alabama.

There are countless tales of that fateful day. Here's our story and what it has to do with breast cancer. School activity ground to a screeching halt after the power went out.

Sure, we'd taught without power before, but this was different. Teachers and students were on edge. We had kept them in the halls for a long time. Then we brought them back into the rooms where they stayed until the buses came. I think we even ate lunch in our classrooms. So far, the day had been hectic, but it had really only just begun.

We rode home, and I took a nap. My wife stayed up, watching live weather coverage on television. She saw footage of the EF-5 tornado that hit Tuscaloosa. That's the town where we both went to college. We found out later that my former apartment complex was decimated. A church just opened by a little league teammate of mine was destroyed the very week it opened for worship. They had a total of one service before the building fell victim to the storm.

The power went out. Electricity seemingly took the last train out of town a couple of hours before the storm hit. Suzette was already in panic mode when I woke up from my nap. I guess she had good reason to react in such a way because the storm that decimated Tuscaloosa was heading our way! Two hours later, we were in the bathtub taking shelter as baseball-sized hail pelted our house.

You'd have thought the funnel cloud was right outside our door. It wasn't. It struck about three miles south of us. It was over in a matter of seconds. We went outside and found the enormous hail scattered all over the yard. Our roof suffered $9,000 worth of damage. We were out of power for a week.

What could we do? Every weatherman in Dixie knew this could be bad and that people would almost certainly die in the carnage.

Cancer is very much like that tornado outbreak of April 27, 2011. A randomly chosen group of the population will acquire the disease. There's little we can do about it.

With the arrival of the tornados, death was literally on our doorstep. Would it destroy our house? Would it destroy our relatives' houses? It was the first time in my life that I knew how a dartboard felt. With Suzette's cancer diagnosis, death is also at our door. Will it spare Suzette? Will it take Suzette? In both cases, it was like death took darts and tossed them to see who lives and who dies. Sure, cancer and tornados only kill a percentage of people. However, their effects are far more reaching than just with whom they kill. Survivors of cancer and tornados may be left damaged, picking up the pieces of their lives in the wake. There is also the fear factor. Just like the whole state cringed with fear while funnel clouds dipped down over the state, a world of people live in fear of developing cancer.

Only God knows who is destined to be a victim of cancer or tornados. We can only duck and hope that we aren't hit. There's little we can do to change that. We just have to wake up every morning, celebrating the sunny days instead of living in fear of the cloudy ones.

Chapter 12

My pastor, Ricky Pollard, delivered a sermon on this passage. I think it is one of the most important scriptures in how it relates to a healthy breast cancer attitude. It's 2 Corinthians 12:7-10, and it says,

"...There was given me a thorn in my flesh, a messenger of Satan, to torment me...I pleaded with the Lord to take it away from me. But he said to me, 'My grace is sufficient for you, for my power is made perfect in weakness.' Therefore I will boast all the more gladly about my weaknesses, so that Christ's power may rest on me. That is why, for Christ's sake, I delight in weaknesses, in insults, in hardships, in persecutions, in difficulties. For when I am weak, then I am strong."

Paul wrote this letter to the church at Corinth. When he mentioned "a thorn in my flesh," the apostle surely didn't have cancer in mind. Many things can dig in and cause torment. Of course, I immediately thought of breast cancer being the thorn in the flesh.

"I pleaded with the Lord to take it away from me. But he said to me, 'My grace is sufficient for you.'" I prayed that Suzette would not have cancer. She and all the other family members did, too. On the surface our prayers appeared to go unanswered. Just because we didn't get what we wanted doesn't mean that God's hand isn't on our family. Satan would tell us that God is far away. We might feel depressed or downtrodden, even lonely because we didn't get what we wanted.

It happens all the time – people not getting what they want. When kids don't get what they want, they pout. We react in a different way. Adults that don't get their way often feel knocked down, defeated, and powerless.

Is giving the child what he/she want what's always best? Of course it isn't. As adults, we have better perspectives…but we don't have God's perspective. Is what we want always what's best for us and for the glory of God? Of course it isn't.

The passage continues, "For my power is made perfect in weakness." God's power is perfect. That we knew, but is it perfect in weakness? Weaknesses, persecutions, and difficulties all seem very far away from God. Do we go to church to feel weakness and difficulties? No. That spiritual high which comes from going to church and studying the Bible gives us an escape from our problems, but that's not all there is to God. Bad things like cancer, like murder, like adultery, like idolatry, all can play a part in the glory of God. God is at work in difficulties - not just when good things come your way.

Paul says that he "boasts all the more gladly about my weaknesses, so that Christ's power may rest upon me." Someone might boast about their weaknesses, hardships, or difficulties in an effort to gain sympathy. I definitely do not think that Paul was doing that. Paul had many difficulties. According to the sermon, he was beaten with a whip, stoned once, and was in a shipwreck three times. Paul used his problems as a witness. His were different from ours, but we can still get comfort from what God does with our problems. He reverses them. He makes them a victory for Him, not a victory for Satan. Praise the fact that you've been given cancer. Praise the fact that you have money troubles. Praise the fact that you've survived a car wreck. Most would curse, not praise these things.

Suzette posted something on Facebook about praying for one of her cousins, who has Crohn's disease. A quick comment marveled at how a person who needs her own prayers was thinking of someone else. Suzette's witness is stronger now than it was before the cancer diagnosis. Paul would say to take advantage of that stronger witness. God is using all situations for His own glory. That's what we're here on earth for anyway.

The scripture continues, "So Christ's power may rest upon me." Christ's power rests upon you when you've coped with your weakness. Just thinking of Christ's power is awe-inspiring. Christ's power is what you want to dwell in. I think it's clear. You don't dwell in that comfort when you're feeling sorry for yourself. You don't dwell in God's comfort when you complain or mope about your situation. What is your witness when you do nothing but complain? Sure, others will give you sympathy, but will that reflect God's glory? No. After all, it's not all about you – even when you're sick. Sickness helps reflect God's glory.

"I delight in weaknesses, in insults, in hardships, in persecutions, in difficulties." God is bigger than your problems. Jesus's death has already won over death. Don't let Satan win. Delight in the hardships that would normally be a victory for Satan.

If I were to sum up this book's sentiment in one sentence, this would be it. "For when I am weak, then I am strong."

Suzette and I have felt weak many times since the cancer diagnosis. The future is decidedly uncertain, but we know that God is using Suzette's illness. Even in sickness, God uses us to reflect His glory. Throughout a time of sickness or hardship is when our witness is at its strongest.

Use it.

Made in the USA
Charleston, SC
10 December 2013